whispers of the trees

poems of love and chaos

CAROLYN ROSSITER

Copyright © 2024 Carolyn Rossiter, All Right Reserved

No part of this document may be reproduced or transmitted in any form or by any means, electronic, mechanical, photocopying, recording or otherwise, without prior written permission from the poet.

Printed in the United States of America

Edited by:
Carolynn Ponzoha and Robert Zweig

Cover and Formatting by:
Michelle Hammer

Dedication

To my brother and all the incredible souls navigating the complexities of life, thank you. Your resilience, courage, and unwavering spirit have not only inspired the creation of this book but have also left an indelible mark on my heart. To those facing the challenges of eating disorders, heartbreak, struggles with alcohol abuse, and the unique journey within the LGBTQIA community, your stories matter, and your strength is immeasurable. This book is a tribute to each of you, a token of gratitude for the shared experiences and the powerful bonds forged in the face of adversity. Thank you for being a source of inspiration, and may these pages echo the collective strength of our shared humanity.

TRIGGER WARNING

On behalf of anyone reading these poems, I would like to add a trigger warning as these stories detail the inner struggles of eating disorders, alcohol abuse, and other kinds of mental abuse. Please take care of yourselves and please read with caution.

POEMS
Sleeves get dirty · 1
I'm only a chapter · 2
Sharing is caring · 3
Addiction · 4
She still cries · 5
Sink in · 6
Dandelions · 7
Haunted · 8
Masking tape · 9
Silent screams · 10
Tattered memories · 11
Bathroom floor · 12
Sunflowers · 13
Going blind · 14
Burning home · 15
Underneath the open sky · 16
In my dreams · 17
Miss you · 18
Pack their bags · 19
Building a wall · 20
Smallest · 21
Fleeting tale · 22
Cold tiles · 23
Blood on my pillow · 24
Chaos · 25
"Diet" · 26
Molded for me · 27
Red door · 28
Salt in my cuts · 29
Found myself · 30
Ripped up pages · 31
Cruel twist · 32

Version of me · 33
Closed the book · 34
Umbrella · 35
Moonlight · 36
Book of love · 37
Another lifetime · 38
Hold onto a memory · 39
Shadows · 40
Turn into art · 41
What if…? · 42
Corners of our hearts · 43
Believe in past lives · 44
Skipping meals · 45
Kisses in hookah bars · 46
Puzzle pieces · 47
Liquor bottles · 48
Dirty mattress · 49
Kisses in taxi cabs · 50
Brain is too tired · 51
Tree House · 52
Ferris-wheel proposal · 53
Work of art · 54
Another weekend with you · 55
Rain · 56
You must have lied · 57
Band Aid · 59
Rest of my life · 60
Felt like art · 61
Door is closed · 62
Sleepwalking · 63
One that got away · 64
Cut me out · 65
You said forever · 66
Entrenched · 67

Remember December · 68
Cold Night · 69
Doormat · 70
Escape · 71
Time and space · 72
Everyone I have ever loved · 73
My own damn mind · 74
Time capsule · 75
See you with her · 76
Let her get away · 77
What could have been · 78
My hands bear scars · 79
Be more · 80
Out of sight · 81
Drowning · 82
Map of your soul · 83
Thunderstorm · 84
Controls you · 85
Dodged a bullet · 86
Not invincible · 87
Beneath the trees · 88
I would be lying · 89
Valley between your bones · 90
Fighting all my life · 91
Keep moving forward · 92
Be my future · 93
Memories that burn · 94
Numbers haunt me · 95
Deck of Cards · 96
Paisley · 97

Sleeves get dirty

My heart is either kept in a cage or worn on my sleeve. There is no middle ground for me. Cages break and sleeves get dirty. Even my heart bruises easily.

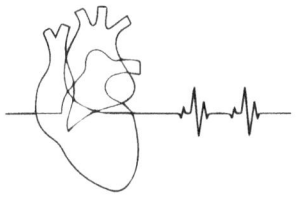

I'm only a chapter

I have always believed I was just a fleeting chapter in everyone's life. Pages turn and people get older. Perhaps I was not even a chapter people read out loud. Just a whispered taboo tale, rarely heard.

Sharing is caring

Sharing is caring but I didn't want to drink the alcohol you fed me in the womb. They say mothers should give their children everything but how can you explain the cocaine you fed me before I even formed a brain. It must be hard to love me more than alcohol.

In the womb, a delicate space of growth and care, A place where love and nourishment should be found everywhere. But sometimes, darkness seeps in, causing pain and despair, Substances that invade, leaving an unborn child unaware.

Addiction

But I'm mourning somebody who hasn't even died and I'm fighting an addiction that isn't even mine.
I watched you fight an illness and I tried to teach myself a lesson with so much reflection.

She still cries

The daughter yells, The mother is angry
the father is gone,
And she will cry

The daughter leaves, The father is back, The husband is back,
And she will cry

The baby is born, The mother is sad, The grandmother is angry,
And now she cries,

The mother leaves,
The baby leaves, The grandmother is calmer,
And she still cries

The baby grows,
The fighting stops, The father doesn't show,
And she still cries

The kids make fun, The doctors call, The stepfather is there,
And she still cries.

Sink in

I have learned that once you make a really bad choice, all the other ones start to sink in afterward. I could not distinguish right from wrong anymore. I just knew that somehow, I wanted to escape and run away from everything.

Dandelions

Just a shy girl in junior high, in a world where other girls longed for boys, my heart yearned for her. I would wish upon dandelions for her to pick me, to notice me. She was a popular girl and we were barely even friends.

At least I realized my heart was meant for feminine souls. Still, society had narrow views. One day, when the world looks less blue and I am a little stronger, I will embrace a love that will feel so true.

Haunted

I used to be haunted by the memories. I know your soul sleeps in tangled thorns, tormented by those you scorned. I have filtered through the chaos as my fears declined. My tattered heart has been rescued by the storm.

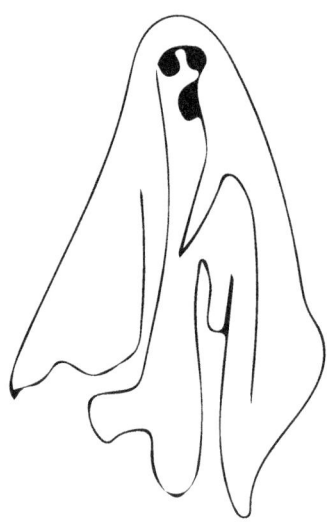

Masking tape

There is masking tape around my waist because my brain tells me rolls are for lazy people. I imagine scissors cutting off the parts of my body that society tells me is not worthy. I'm always too loud and I talk too fast.

I stole diet pills because you told me to. I had one hand around my hair and one down my throat because you made me think it was the only way.

Silent screams

The mirror reflects a fractured soul, Ravaged by urges, beyond control.

Erosion whispers with each purging tide,
A tempest within, where secrets hide.
Silent screams in the night replay.
Weighted hearts, a heavy toll

Teeth worn thin, enamel fades away,
Stomach's rebellion, night and day.
In the hollow echoes of self-betrayal.
Digestive whispers, secrets unfold,
In the depths where darkness take

A fragile vessel bearing invisible scars and the torment within In pursuit of an elusive, haunting goal.

Tattered memories

I have a museum of tattered memories...
and I've been through a blizzard of insults,
but you have given me a garden of hope.

Bathroom floor

There is nothing beautiful about the feeling of cold tiles as you sit on the bathroom floor. There is nothing sexy about the cuts on your knuckles and the bruises on your body. There is nothing charming about your glands swelling up so much you look like a fish. Nothing brings you back to reality. You're afraid to die but all you can do is cry. You tell yourself that you can not do this anymore.

Being tiny won me no prizes. Instead it gave me some nasty surprises. The coldness you feel is hard to explain. It surrounds your bones and ceases your brain. Being starving isn't pretty or elegant. In truth it's really quite gloomy.

 Suddenly realizing that thin isn't bliss There is a proper life that we're all going to miss. Crawl out of this hole before it's too late. This miserable existence isn't your fate.

Sunflowers

I planted sunflowers with the monsoon life poured my way.
They bathed in raindrops and emerged from the soil.
A tapestry of golden petals, dancing in the breeze.

Flowers grew in spite as the tempestuous storms swept through.
Roots anchored deep, resilient and strong, absorbing the tears of the sky, thriving all along.

Going blind

At just Sixteen, darkness claimed my brother's eyes.
A hushed sorrow whispered through the skies.
A silent thief, a cruel twist of destiny.
A world once vibrant, now obscured.
Leaving me, at twenty-nine, burdened with fear.

But through time, I learned, in the midst of my brother's fight,
That anxiety, though fierce, can be put to flight,
For within darkness, we may find our way,
And in surrendering, discover a brighter day.

With the loss of his fight, he gained a perception of beauty in the world .
His fingertips danced and explored new realms.
He never let his heart get bitter.
He now knows more about my soul than my looks.
He taught me to appreciate listening more and
love myself for who I am.

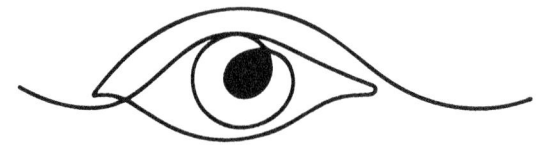

Burning home

I wanted to make a home out of you.
The way you make me feel,
it didn't always feel warm and welcoming,
but I looked for you in every stranger's face.

When the nights got cold and your arms were not there to hold,
I felt the roof caving in.

It is like walking back into a burning building after being rescued.
It is painful, however, after the smoke clears, it is the only thing
that feels like home.

Underneath the open sky

Underneath the open sky, in the backseat of that old jeep,
Memories etched in the fabric of time,
Our love blossomed, wild and free,
In that secret place, hopefully not a crime

Do you remember, my love, those cherished nights,
When time stood still, and our hearts aligned,

Driving in your jeep, to the park we'd stray,
Those were my favorite times, oh, what a time.

The songs playing, serenaded our hearts,
As we bared our souls in whispered words,
Passions ignited, flames embraced,
Creating a symphony only we ever heard.

Moments into memories,
Wrapped in an embrace,
The park transformed into a sacred space,
Where our hearts found solace and grace.

Oh, the sweet nostalgia floods my mind,
As I reminisce about the love we shared,
Those stolen hours, forever enshrined,
In the depths of my soul, eternally declared.

In my dreams

And I wrote to you in my dreams, wishing upon stars to get back feelings I couldn't see, in fear of forever losing something that meant so much to me.

Miss you

She said, "I miss you" without context. Smiled without her eyes. Laughed with her lips closed. Spoke with no sound. All I have are the tears I try not to cry.

Pack their bags

And I write down every word I am too afraid to say out loud. You won't stick around for more than a couple of rounds. I know because I get tired of myself too. People pack their bags when they tire of me. I wish I could leave myself too.

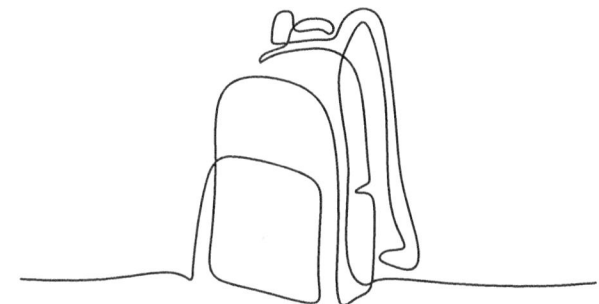

Building a wall

In the process of protecting my heart, I have broken yours. In the wake of trying to save my pride, I have burnt a hole into yours. And by building a wall to keep our love safe, the wall is now a prison.

And maybe, just maybe my fear that you are out with someone more secure and worthy of your love will actually give you the courage to go out and find her.

Smallest

Even at my smallest, I was not the happiest.
I realized I was still insecure when I was thin.

Fleeting tale

From the moment we met, I have a room in my heart with memories we made. You craved a fleeting tale, I yearned for an epic, in my hands, a novel woven. So you shred yours but I still have mine on paper, whispering through time. I will read our story over and over again because it's the only place I have you now.

I told you, in ten years time, you would still be on my mind. You and I have moved on and I am just a chapter in your life, but for me, you will always be the entire story.

I wish I could repeat the day we met, over and over again. Please give me the chance to write us another chapter. Ten thousand more chapters.

So I gave you what I wanted and I sat alone every night, reading the pages of our story, obsessively trying to fill the void you left inside of me. Now she gets the entire book of stories with you and I am left with just the memories in my head.

Cold tiles

There is nothing beautiful about the feeling of cold tiles as you sit on the bathroom floor. There is nothing sexy about the cuts on your knuckles and the bruises on your knees. There is nothing charming about your glands swelling up so much you look like a fish. Nothing brings you back to reality. You're afraid to die but all you can do is cry. You tell yourself that you can not do this anymore.

Blood on my pillow

The sun did not yet rise as I woke to the sight of blood on my pillow and spilling from my mouth. A taste of copper, metallic and bitter, lingers on my tongue as I look down at the stains on my sheets. More haunting reminders. Years of self abuse screaming in my ears. I felt scared but accomplished. The only self harm that people are congratulated for.

Calling my roommate and her girlfriend for help. Running up to the bathroom to wash out my mouth. Scaring myself by looking in the mirror and seeing the blood on my teeth and slipping off my tongue. Look at what you have done?

So we drove to the hospital. After some tests, the doctor told me I needed to change. No more drinking 5 cups of coffee a day. My past with self induced vomiting and drinking alcohol instead of eating food, came back to punish me. My body was rebelling against me. At the same time, I felt accomplished. This is what the eating disorder does. It makes you think, the sicker you are, the more you have won.

Chaos

There is comfort in the madness. I was brainwashed to believe that love was destruction and I felt safe in the chaos.

"Diet"

An innocent "diet" is how it starts.
Before you know it, it will hit you like darts.
Destructive thoughts and extreme panic.
Being forced to eat will feel tragic.

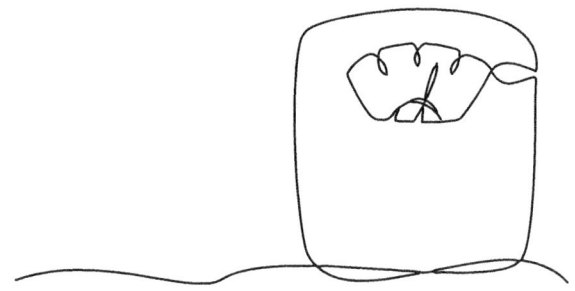

Molded for me

Her hand molded into mine as if two potters made them out of clay. I can still feel her body move against mine, moving like water in an infinite dance. Every move was animated by the love we had for each other.

I was
Constructed
for you,
and you
were molded
for me.

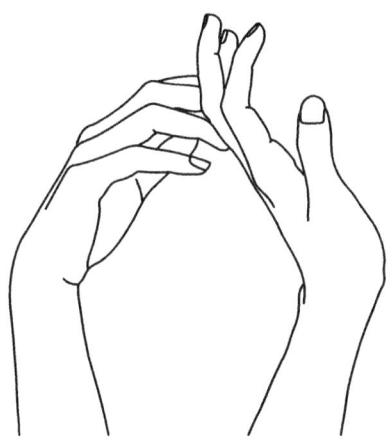

Red door

You said, "One day, I will buy you a typewriter, for all your beautiful thoughts, and we will sip wine in front of our house with the red door and I will sing you the songs on my record player."

Of all the pictures I have painted in my mind, ours is by far the prettiest.

Behind the red door was supposed to be the number 28. Imagines of what could have been, flooding through the house. So many whispers made time fly away. Behind that door, my heart would hold all of the stories untold. Now regrets echo in the silence.

Salt in my cuts

You brought me the ocean with my open wounds. You called me dramatic as the salt seeped into my cuts. I took you back because you were always there with a towel to dry me off.

She made me bleed but she always healed the wounds.
I hope the bruises never fade along with the memories we made.

Found myself

And for once in that moment, I have forgotten what pain feels like. In that small moment, I found myself.

Ripped up pages

You ripped up every page and burned the pieces to the ground,
Through the raging fires and scattered pages,
Our story remains. In the ashes of love's goodbye,
I preserve our tale, a cherished lullaby.

Amidst crystals and photos of us in nature's embrace,
Our book remains a sacred space.
For on the shelf of memories kept,
Our love story lingers, never to be swept.

If you fall in love with a writer,
know that your essence will live on, long after your relationship ends.

Someday, if anyone asks me whether I knew you,
I will tell them that you were the best love story I ever read.

Cruel twist

In vulnerability, strength is found,
A gentle echo, a healing sound.
In shadows danced the hidden pain,
A silent struggle, not in vain.
Bulimia's grasp, a cruel twist,
Leaves scars unseen, a silent tryst.

Version of me

Maybe I don't miss you anymore but I miss the version of me that I was when I was with you. I was spirited and my face lit up like a little kid on Christmas every time I saw you and I sure miss the passion I had for life when you were in mine.

Closed the book

You closed the book, but the movie keeps playing in the back of my mind.

Umbrella

It felt as though we were sharing one umbrella for years. Just running through the storm of life together. As time went on our umbrella began to break. We could no longer keep each other safe and warm, but I still smile every time it rains.

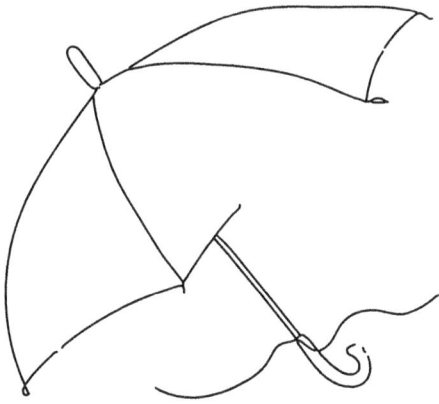

Moonlight

Moonlight weaves regrets, a silken thread,
She left, taking both my heart and what was left unsaid.
In echoes of laughter and promises broken, I will hide my tears
and leave my feelings unspoken.

Book of love

In our book of love, a bookmark placed,
She left my heart, emotions laced.
A tale I know to be unfinished, echoes stray,
She walked away, but memories stayed.

Another lifetime

You were my soulmate, but maybe we were made to be in another lifetime.

Hold onto a memory

And even after all this time, even after realizing how much damage was done; If I could go back in time, I would go to any day we were still together. Laying in bed, wrapped in each other's fragile arms, feeling each other's heartbeats, feeling each other's breath. I would give anything to hear her laugh one more time. Going back to our adventures, believing it was us against the world. Tell me...how long do you hold onto a memory? How do you decide to choose between the pain of remembering versus the pain of letting go? For me, I was more afraid to forget the memories.

Shadows

In the shadows of the past, a ghostly silhouette,
A memory of sickness, a time I can't forget.
Too skinny, too frail, a body worn and thin,

The frailty, the fragility, a twisted kinship, Missing the sick body, a peculiar relationship. In the struggle, there was a strange allure, A dance with darkness, though it wasn't pure.

The tiny frame, a twisted kind of grace, now missed in the present, a haunted space.

In the echoes, a yearning begins.
The mirror reflects a healthier me,
But sometimes, nostalgia longs for what used to be.

Turn into art

I'll write down all the words I'm not allowed to say to you.
I wrote down every mistake I've made and turned it into a book.
I turned the way you left into poetry.

What if...?

What if we met a little later? What if we met when we were a little older and you were done with school and I had time to find myself? You had to make sure that there was no one else out there for you. I already knew, you were my only.

What if we met before you decided to go away to school? What if we were never long distance? Maybe we would have been different and would feel lucky to be able to settle down so young.

You had your plans and I would not be the jenga block being pulled from your tower in a game that was only half way done. In my heart, our game had only just begun.

What if we could go back in time and meet again? I would run through the darkest parts of my memories if that is what it took for us to try again. I know we would work this time.

What if we met a little later? Would you have been definite in your feelings ?

I would have met you anywhere, sooner or later, in this lifetime or another and I would have been sure every time.

Corners of our hearts

In the quiet corners of our hearts,
there is someone that lies almost unspoken
That even hearing their name makes your soul tremble with
memories and pain. Someone who makes my heartbreak a little
more each time I hear your song.

Their significance is immeasurable.
Mention of their name causes a tremor in the soul,
Memories and pain intertwined, an emotional toll.

Your song, a haunting melody, echoes their ghost,
Each note, a reminder,
With every refrain, a little more my heart aches,
A symphony of longing, a love that never forsakes.

Believe in past lives

In another time and place, we were entwined
In a love that transcends all boundaries
I can feel it in my soul, a memory so vivid
A love that burned like a fiery flame

I must have known you in a past life
For the connection between us is so strong
I believe we were soulmates, destined to find each other
Time and time again, in different forms

I swear I can hear the echoes of our laughter
And feel the warmth of your embrace
In another time, we were more
Of a love that could not be erased

So here we are, in this lifetime
But I know that our souls have met before
I must believe in past lives, for I can't shake this feeling
That you and I were once something more

Skipping meals

Skipping meals and taking pills,
It was like running through sand,
Gravel digging into my spine.
I made a bed out of rubble,
Acid in my throat, a constant reminder.

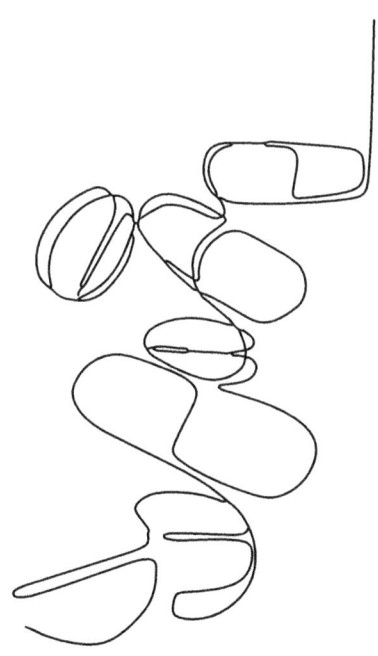

Kisses in hookah bars

In a dimly lit hookah bar in NYC,
Where smoke swirls with the sound of laughter in the air,
My childhood friend arrived, with a guest in tow.
I didn't feel like being with an extra person
But little did I know, this night would bring unexpected changes.

Conversation flowed like the alcohol into our glasses.
There was a flicker in her eyes and a playful smile.
A girl so enchanting that time stood still.

Our lips met as a dare in the drinking game we had all been playing. My first kiss with a girl.
Never will I forget that fleeting touch. To them, it was just a game.
To me, nothing will ever be the same.

For that kiss, so short and tender, inscribed a truth I tried to pretend didn't exist. Never will I kiss a man again. My heart yearns for a different end.

Puzzle pieces

Our trauma shaped us perfectly like a puzzle, but what an ugly picture we were creating.

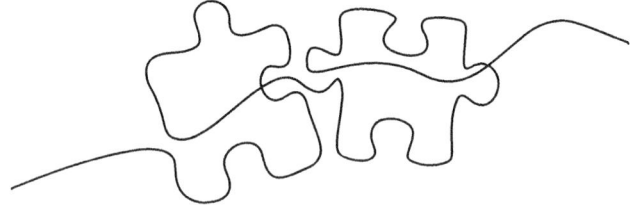

Liquor bottles

Liquor bottles hidden in my closet. My dreams shattered like the bottles we broke. Can I bloom in a haunted room? I built the ruins and I created this dust.

Dirty mattress

It is the best friend in my life, that I cannot cut out of my life.
This abusive relationship I cannot get out of.
It's even like the alcoholic father I cannot stop enabling,
Even like the broken home that I cannot leave,
Like the dirty mattress, I cannot stop sleeping on.

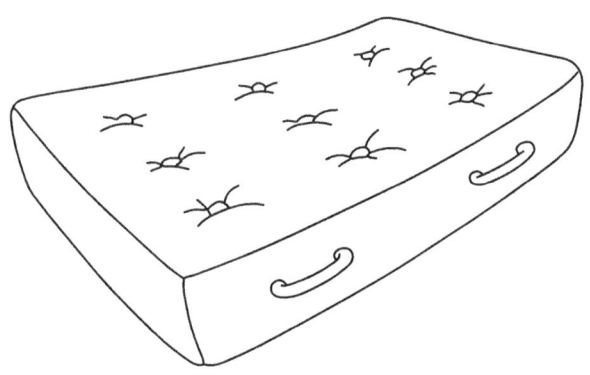

Kisses in taxi cabs

In taxi cabs through city streets we roam,
A tipsy waltz, the city as our home.
Under city lights,
Drunk kisses bloom on intoxicated nights.

Raindrops tap the windows, a rhythmic beat,
As laughter spills and lips inebriated meet.
Sipping on vodka and iced tea as we make our way home
Street Lights flicker, reflecting on the glass,
As intoxicated love makes the moments pass.

Brain is too tired

It's so dark but my brain is too tired to keep looking for the light. Sleeping too much but not enough.

Tree House

And you've wrapped them up and thrown them to the sky
Will you walk the river where we used to hide?
Will you find me by the tree house we once hiked to and carved our initials into?

Ferris-wheel proposal

You asked me to marry you on that ferris-wheel wheel in little Italy. I wish I had said yes. City hall is not too far away.

If I close my eyes, I can picture the life we would be living now if I grabbed your hand and said let's go.

She needed that big yellow diamond ring but you know I would have taken a piece of string. You can marry her. You can build a life but that won't stop you from thinking about that day.

Work of art

I have so much of you in my heart. A love story etched, a work of art.

Another weekend with you

Another weekend in PA with you.
You just dropped me off at the bus stop.
In the parking lot, I sat alone,
Awaiting the bus to take me back home to NY.
Recalling the moments, her hand in mine,
Bittersweet tears flowed freely, like a glass of wine.
Already counting down the days until we are together again.

Rain

Nothing knows me better than the rain. Each drop holds a memory. I still remember the two of us walking you to the train at six in the morning. We were holding hands and laughing with rain dripping down our faces. You grabbed my face with both of your hands and kissed me.

In this garden of memories, rain is pouring down as we kiss around the flowers. Whispers of time, and a fading melody. You took my hand, took a chance and we took a step into life's dance. Through winding roads, we will find our way, with love, come what may.

You must have lied

You must have lied when you said that you were in it for the long haul. It must have been the alcohol.

I believed in your promises, in the whispers of forever. But now see the truth unfold, In the empty spaces between us, In the silence that fills the room, In the cracks of broken dreams.

You must have lied when you said you would hold on tight,
For your grip has loosened, and I am left drifting away in fright.
The love we shared, a fleeting flame, Once ablaze,
now extinguished,

Leaving only ashes of what once was,
Scattered remnants of a broken vow.

You must have lied when you said you were committed, dedicated, For your words were hollow, Echoing in the chambers of my heart.

I trusted you, believed in us, but now I know the truth, that your love was temporary, A mirage in the desert of my longing.

Your words were promises etched in stone, that now crumble, disintegrate and dissolve into the unknown. Leaving me to grapple with the weight of your deceit, a heavy burden I never thought I would meet.

"I keep us neatly packed in a box inside my heart." That is what you told me. That is what I believed.

Falling for you felt like my scared soul lit up with a thousand candles. until the lights started to flicker, you turned me into a shadow

I felt so alive until you left me to burn.
You loved igniting the flame and I learned to love the liar.
You must have lied when you said you were in this for the long haul.

Band Aid

I have been treating you like a band aid, when you might actually be the wound.

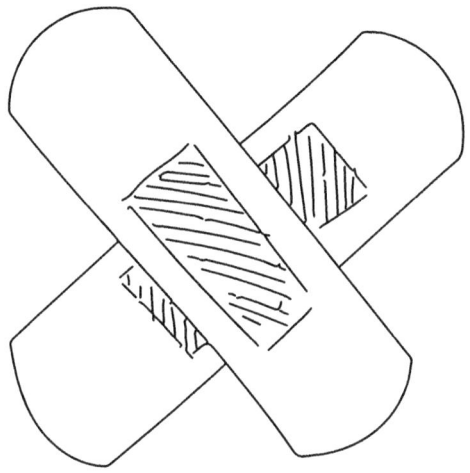

Rest of my life

Half of the time I find myself wondering how I was so blind to what was truly right in front of my face the entire time. The other half is spent trying to figure out how I'm going to spend the rest of my life without ever again feeling the way only you made me feel.

Felt like art

Let me remind me what we had before you tear it all down. My heart that was once so full is now torn apart. Our story no longer feels like art.

I kept time in worn pages so I could keep each embrace. My old journals were my safe space

Door is closed

Your door is closed.
I am not fighting
to be let back in,
and you do not stay close enough
on the other side
to hear if I even tried.
but my soul will visit
the memories
we made
for lifetimes to come

Sleepwalking

I've been sleep walking my entire life until I met you. Sometimes I think I must have only dreamt of you this entire time.

I guess it was all in my mind.

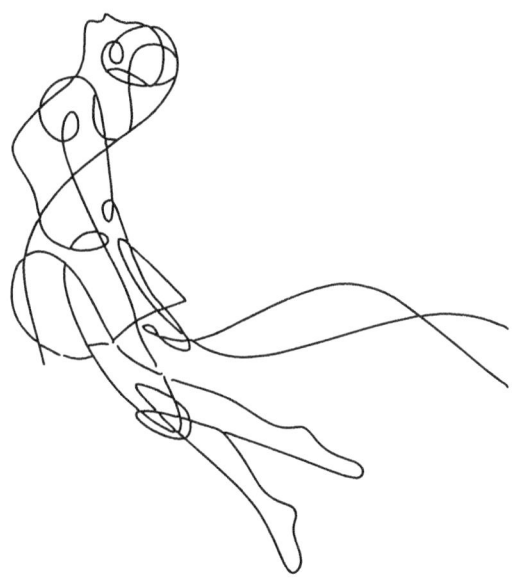

One that got away

These words reveals the scars I can't erase,
A silent plea for another embrace.
In every sentence, a bittersweet trace,
Lingering moments of the one that got away

Storms of joy clash with waves of despair.
Tears, like raindrops, fall in a fleeting dance.
I told you, no one else can compare.

Among the trails, whispers of pine sway
Mountains echoed tales from our long ago days.
Footprints etched in soil, just like the one that got away.

Cut me out

Out of all the people in my life, you were the last person I ever expected to cut me out.

You said forever

You said forever and I bought it. You said goodbye and I fought it. I miss you calling me yours and holding you in your grad school apartment.

"I keep us neatly packed in a box inside my heart." That is what you told me. That is what I believed.

You packed us up in a box with no bow. Who are we now? I have imagined this
story before. In my mind, you never walked out the door.

But there was no knock on my door, no sorry for the mess we made. I will write myself the letters because you don't read them anymore.

In another life, you would show up with that box of our memories. A box full of old photos from our time together, CDs, stuffed animals, rose petals, concert tickets and wine corks. We would place them on our mantle and one day tell our grandkids about our love story. I thought all we needed was some time apart and then we could start all over.

Entrenched

It was like you woke up one day and decided I was no longer what you wanted. Stories of us will forever be written in my heart. The way you made me feel will always be entrenched within my soul. She has woven herself in every fiber of my being.

Remember December

It was late December and I can still remember the cold wind hitting my face. It was so long ago but if I close my eyes, I can still feel you as we cuddled at our place.

I still remember us dancing in your grad school apartment. String of lights around your bed. The playlist you made for us still exists in my mind. Can you still reach for my hand and tell me it's your favorite story too?

And if you close your eyes, can you still picture us drinking wine and eating chocolate on your parents roof?

Don't forget. I'll never forget the long drives and your sweet brown eyes. Please keep at least one memory in your back pocket.

Cold Night

You were a warm shoulder on a cold night. I saw a light in you. I saw magic in us. I still remember your tan skin and the way your lips twitched in your sleep.

I still hear your laugh and see the way you cared for others. If only the timing was right, because we became a cold shoulder on a warm night.

Doormat

You say I seem different.
You say I've changed since we broke up.
I am no longer your doormat.
I am no longer willing to accept all the negative things you have told me just so you will stay in my life.

Escape

On the couch I lay, for months on end,
The bed, a haunting reminder of a love I could not mend.
Images of us, a vivid, haunting
Playing like a movie, taunting my heart.

Bags already packed, a silent vow,
I boarded a bus, an escape somehow.
To another state, a journey to reset,
A quest for peace, and a chance to at least pretend to forget.

Time and space

You wanted time and space. I don't know where I am going but I am not where you left me.

Please show up at my door and let the memories unfold. Bring our box of moments and let's get excited about all the untold. Echoes of laughter, whispers of grace. Time suspended in a familiar space.

Everyone I have ever loved

I carry memories from everyone I have ever loved. Some of them I protect and wish I could go back to some day. Some now belong in my past and wish the best for. Some I wish could just forget after I have helped someone else with the lessons they have learned from them. Instead, I will forever be haunted by every sigh, every love you and every argument.

My own damn mind

The hardest thing I ever had to fight, is my own damn mind. It walks into the same room trying to fix the broken floorboards and paint the chipped walls.

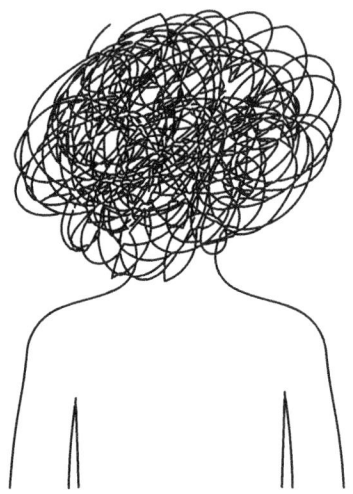

Time capsule

Years later, we met again. It was like stepping into a time capsule. I knew we were meeting but it still felt like fate. I walked straight to the past's embrace.

I pulled the curtain and there you were.
Wished I asked for a longer hug. Your hand in my hand felt so familiar. Like a key unlocking memories of long ago. Bringing me back to the day we met, when our love story had yet to unfold.

But there you stood, with a new love by your side, and there I was, with mine by mine. My heart, still wounded, still bleeding, longing for a chance to intertwine again.

Pick me, I thought in my head, along with all the other unspoken words. I believed we could work this time. Mend the fractures and fly like free birds. In that moment, time stood still as ghosts from the past danced with hope and uncertainty.

Beneath the surface, emotions stirred, and even though I longed for your touch, reality whispered, "it would be absurd". Fate's path was already set, leaving us to wonder.

So we part ways with bittersweet smiles and a final glance. Seeing a love that was once mine. Life moves on and so must we, even though I yearn for that sign. I carry the echoes of a love that could have been, I guess never stood a chance.

See you with her

I am not that strong. I can not stand to see you with her. Even though it's been so long.

Let her get away

You don't want 50 years to go by and then realize you let the love of your life get away. I never changed my mind about you. I tried to, but it just wouldn't ever work. There's something about us. Something inside me just won't let you go. The one person l could be myself around. The one person who really understood me. The person I would talk with until four am. The one person that got excited about the little things with me. The one person that made me so happy that laughed in my sleep. The one person I wanted to be a mother with. Travel with. wake up every morning and drink coffee with. The one person that helped me breathe when I was having a bad day. The one person that could make me laugh no matter what.

Now someone else is watching you sleep. Someone else is making you coffee in the morning. Someone else is taking you to museums and laughing with you. Someone else is holding your hand and kissing your lips. Someone else is calling you pet names and hanging out with you and your friends. Someone else is making you so happy that you might laugh in your sleep. Someone else is your new best friend. And I have to learn to accept that. You deserve to be happy. I have to leave you alone and let go of the greatest love I have ever known.

What could have been

In words, I sought the echoes of the past,
The one that slipped away too fast.
Her laughter lingers in the midnight air,
A ghostly whisper, my favorite love affair.

Through the pages, my heart's inked refrain,
A melody of joy, a touch of pain.
The one that got away, a ghostly muse,
In every line, her memory I choose

A wistful stroke of what could have been,
A tapestry of love, lost within the pen.

My hands bear scars

Our fingers used to be woven together. Now my hands bear scars that I don't even recognize. Marks of separation

Be more

They compliment my weight but they don't notice the fat that I do? Can't they see that I'm a work in progress? Can they not tell that I needed to weigh less?

Weigh less so I could be more. Be more and feel less. These secret skills I harbored might not be secrets after all. Do they notice all I have endured? I do not want a cure. No, I want to be seen.
I'm afraid of dying but I want to be close to death. I feel accomplished in the worries of others. I want people to notice but I don't want them to help.

Out of sight

I'm still in love with old memories of you and I. Out of sight is not always out of mind.

Drowning

I was turning into someone I didn't like. I couldn't fit all of the trauma in one boat. I found myself in chapters of grief and saved myself from drowning.

CAROLYN ROSSITER

Map of your soul

Somewhere in this fucked up world, there must exist a map to your soul one that would lead me back to you. the real you; the you that I caught a glimpse of so long ago.

Two souls entwined, disappeared by fear. Time rewinds as you put your hand in mine.

We were still unchanged in life's dance. I keep wishing to go back to the last day I saw you. Lingering in your stares embrace. Take me back to the fire burning home.

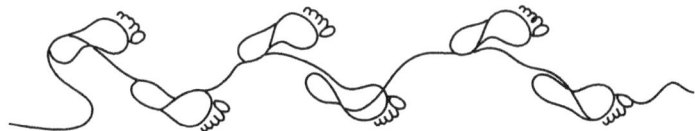

Thunderstorm

Missing you is like a thunderstorm. It is loud, heavy and sometimes unexpected. Everything around me is turning gray because I don't remember how to see in color. I look out the window and wonder when it will stop. all this hurting all this grief. all this darkness. The truth is, I don't think the rain is leaving anytime soon. the truth is,

I will miss you even when the power comes back on.

Controls you

I would say, the most profound relationship I have had in my life is with the one that made me so familiar with my fingertips and the acid in my throat. The relationship that makes me feel guilty for putting any type of food in my body. The one that draws me in every time something stressful happens. There is a comfort in the pain. A comfort in thinking I have control of something in my life. The somber truth is, you do not have control when you have an eating disorder. The eating disorder controls you.

Dodged a bullet

Months of trying to heal each other. In the end we turned each other into versions of ourselves we could not recognize. Everyone thinks I dodged a bullet but who held the gun?

Not invincible

When we are young, we think we are invincible. Rationalizing bad habits over and over again. Never believing our actions would affect us as we get older.

The more my body fell apart, the more I realized how wrong I was. The more I thought about how long I spent hating my body, the more I learned to love it.

Beneath the trees

Our stories began beneath the trees. I think I've come to terms with the fact that there will always be branches of loneliness running through who I am.

I found myself beneath the trees as I weeped with the changing leaves and the river called my name at night. Whispered so lightly.

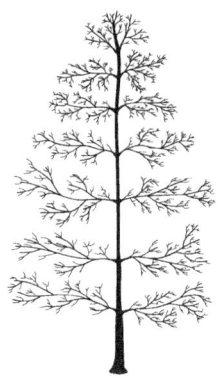

I would be lying

I wish I was normal. I wish I didn't miss my ribs sticking out. I wish I didn't miss my face when it wasn't as round. Instead of being happy for healing, I am angry that I need to.

I would be lying if I said it didn't affect my mood anymore. I would be lying if I said I didn't still think about it a hundred times a day. I would be lying, if I said I didn't miss being able to count my ribs and play the drums on my hip bones. I would be lying if I said I no longer crave seeing my collarbones clearly outlined.

I would be lying if I said I no longer feel pride when I sleep instead of eat I would be lying, if I said there are are not moments where I have to try so hard not to cry on the fucking floor of the bathroom. I would be lying, if I said I no longer feel like I am drowning.

Valley between your bones

If you think you'll find a home in the valleys between your bones, trust me you'll only end up alone.

I have seen all I care to see of you
You have no more to offer me
No longer feel comforting
You no longer feel like home

Fighting all my life

Tears linger in my once tortured throat and I miss the way I used to get rid of them. Instead, there is silent scream and a fear of shattered dreams.

I no longer cry on the fucking floor of the bathroom but I still fight the words in my brain. It is a war I have been fighting all of my life.

Keep moving forward

If there is anything I have learned in the years filled with chaos, it is that no matter how many bridges are burned behind you, you must keep moving forward. Respect yourself enough to walk away from something that no longer helps you grow or make you happy.

Be my future

I will erase my past if you will be my future.

Memories that burn

There are memories that still burn in my mind, like the acid in my throat. There are also parts of my life that I can not remember, and maybe that is for the best. I may have developed an affinity for pain. There is comfort in the familiar.

Numbers haunt me

Numbers haunt me and tell me I am not enough. I was not good at math but I always knew how much I lost or gained. I had a hard time focusing in school but I could focus on how much I should exercise.

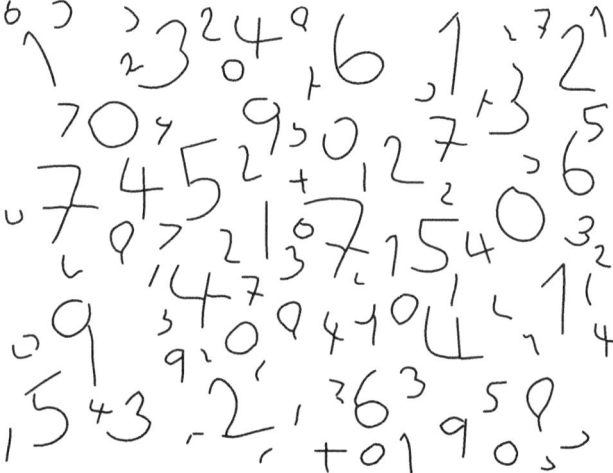

Deck of Cards

I was dealt with a deck of cards that turned me into something I had never imagined. Something I was not prepared for but in the end, it made me stronger.

Paisley

My dog Paisley is my best friend. She will be a loyal companion until the very end. It is a bond that can never mend. With her wagging tail and gentle eyes that I swear are human, she brings me joy that will never die. Through changing seasons, come what may, I know you are here to stay.

About The Author

Raised in New York City, Carolyn finds joy in writing, hiking, and cherishing moments with her wife, Michelle, and their dog, Paisley. As an advocate for eating disorder awareness and LGBTQIA rights, Carolyn channels her lived experiences to educate and inspire others through her words.

Other Works

Diet Pills and Broken Dreams | Stories I Could Not Tell
- A Memoir

You can find Carolyn on Instagram at:

@_breatheinhopeandpoetry

Printed in Great Britain
by Amazon